PAULA DEEN'S

Kitchen Wisdom
AND RECIPE JOURNAL

PAULA DEEN

with SHERRY SUIB COHEN

Simon & Schuster

NEW YORK · LONDON · TORONTO · SYDNEY

Simon & Schuster
1230 Avenue of the Americas
New York, NY 10020

First Simon & Schuster hardcover edition November 2008

SIMON & SCHUSTER and colophon are registered trademarks
of Simon & Schuster, Inc.

For information about special discounts for bulk purchases,
please contact Simon & Schuster Special Sales at
1-800-456-6798 or business@simonandschuster.com.

Designed by Jaime Putorti

Manufactured in the United States of America

1   3   5   7   9   10   8   6   4   2

Library of Congress Cataloging-in-Publication Data
Deen, Paula H.
Paula Deen's kitchen wisdom and recipe journal / Paula Deen ; with Sherry Suib Cohen.
p. cm.
1. Cookery—Miscellanea.
I. Cohen, Sherry Suib. II. Title.
TX652.D437 2008
641.5—dc22   2008029367

ISBN-13: 978-1-4165-9702-5
ISBN-10:   1-4165-9702-6

To Corrie Hiers,
child of my heart and daughter of my darlin' baby brother, Bubba.
I love this beautiful girl, my momma's namesake and my joy.
She provides loyalty, comic relief, and always
the best company for me and Michael.

PAULA DEEN'S

AND RECIPE JOURNAL

A WORD FROM PAULA

When I was little, I learned to cook mainly from my Grand-momma Paul. She was a masterful cook, but more than that, she loved me, and the wise words she gave me about how she felt about cookin' and how to ripen fruits and break bread and fix the occasional cookin' calamity were far more important than even her wonderful recipes. I wish I'd had a kind of journal then, to write down all those grand-momma-wise words along with my own ideas that popped up as I watched her chop pecans for her fresh apple cake. My best thoughts on life still seem to appear when I'm stirrin' my pots, and the freshest impressions and even the sweetest memories of family and friends come bubblin' up along with the intoxicatin' smells from the jambalaya on my stove.

Take this old story I heard when I was very small. There was this young wife who asked her momma why the momma always cut a little bit offin' the butt end of a pork roast before she cooked it. Because, the momma explained, it tastes better because the juices are released easier and because her momma cooked it that way and because *her* momma did the same.

The young woman wasn't convinced and she traveled a long way to ask the identical question of her grandmomma.

The old woman thought and thought, trying to remember, and finally she said, "I cut off the butt end because how else would I fit the durn potatoes around it?"

This journal, then, is my way of getting some of my personal solutions, some new recipes, and passed-on tips to you and still give you room for the potatoes. The blank pages are for you to jot down your own answers to cookin' dilemmas and recipes you've learned and adapted from your momma and want to pass down to your kids. It's also for you to write your own flights of fancy, inventions, frustrations, and victories in the kitchen—a cookin' diary to look back on and laugh and remember your signature dish that you made every weekend when the kids were little but you haven't made in years.

I'm hopin' you take pleasure in some of my personal reflections, and, more than anything, I'm also hopin' that you enjoy collaborating with me in your own kitchen. If you really let loose and write down your deepest feelings about cookin' and family and kitchen memories, I'm banking on it that you'll jump on this cookin' journal like a duck on a June bug.

IT AIN'T ROCKET SCIENCE

*D*on't take cookin' too seriously, girl. Life gets hard soon as we walk out our doors; cookin' should not be hard. Look: If you love challenges and lean toward the gourmet world (that ain't me, though), by all means, lean in all the way. But when all is said and done, the bottom line is that your best dishes are the uncomplicated dishes you yourself like, not those you're trying to impress people with.

But what if you get in there and you really do ruin a meal? Well, it ain't the end of the world and hopefully it ain't your last meal. Throw it in the trash and order takeout.

The largest item on any menu in the world is probably the

roast camel served at Bedouin weddings. The camel is

stuffed with a sheep, which is stuffed with chickens, which

are stuffed with fish, which are stuffed with eggs.

Kind of like my turducken.

HOW DO I . . . ?

▪ Slice an onion so I only cry a little?

Wet the onion (and your hands) and let the cold water run hard while you slice that baby on a cuttin' board. Some folks slice the onion right under the stream of cold water; others wear goggles. Some others burn two or three candles near the cuttin' board, because the flames seem to send the onion-smelly air up in smoke. If you're cookin' with gas, you can position your cuttin' board near a couple of turned-on gas burners and slice away without cryin' hardly a tear.

Personally, I mostly swear by holdin' an unlit wooden matchstick in my teeth when slicin' onions—the match head facin' out, please.

▪ Skim the fat off the soup stock?

Easy. Pour your stock into containers and refrigerate it, covered, for about two to three hours, or put the containers in the freezer for about thirty minutes. When you get out those containers, that fat will have risen right to the top and solidified for you to peel right off, nice and easy, with your slotted spoon!

If you don't mind messy and need to degrease right away, place a layer of paper towels over the surface of the warm soup: The towels will sop up some of the fat. Lift the paper off and immediately discard the fatty towel in a plastic trash bag. Repeat and repeat again until all the fat is skimmed off the soup.

Lettuce leaves work great, too. Just swirl a couple of clean lettuce leaves over the top of the soup, then discard. Repeat with fresh leaves until the surface is to your liking.

Or try dragging a couple of ice cubes in a slotted spoon over the top of the soup; the fat will adhere to the cubes.

▪ Get rid of the smell after I fry fish?

If the kitchen smells like somethin' the dog's been keepin' him under the porch, opening the windows just won't do it, girl. For a fish-stinky room, put out a heated bowl of white vinegar on the counter. Or try rubbin' down your cuttin' board, knife, and pan with lemon juice. A small glass bowl of bleach placed somewhere in the room—up high, on top of the refrigerator or a cabinet so a pet or child doesn't accidentally drink it—makes that fishi-

ness go away like nothing else. And for a fishy-smelling fridge, an open box of bicarbonate of soda left on a shelf overnight works wonders.

■ Discourage bugs from takin' up residence in my flour?

Place a few whole bay leaves in tightly lidded plastic flour, cereal, or cornmeal containers. Sometimes I put the flour and the bay leaves into plastic bags and store the closed bags in the freezer or refrigerator until I'm ready to use them.

A friend of mine claims that the critters hate sulphur the way bad smells hate sulphur, and the way to make weevils scarce as hen's teeth is to lay a pack of matches right on top of the flour in the container. Works for her.

■ Fix it that the whippin' cream don't turn to butter?

For the best whipped cream, thoroughly whip chilled heavy cream (make sure it ain't half-and-half) with a whisk, a handheld mixer, or a stand mixer. I chill my whisk or beaters in the refrigerator for about twenty minutes. The whipped cream is done when the cream comes to cloud-like, firm peaks that stand up pretty straight and proud, not mushy peaks that flop over when the beaters are lifted. But go slow, honey—a little bit too much whippin', and you've got a topping for your English muffin, not for your hot fudge sundae. In other words, you got butter.

If you've overwhipped just a tiny bit and the cream hasn't yet quite separated and actually turned to butter, turn off the mixer, add a few more tablespoons of the heavy cream, and finish whippin' with a hand whisk.

■ Skin a chicken without cursing?

Used to be, I couldn't. First of all, it's damn hard to get that slippery skin off, and second, the skin is one of my most favorite parts of the eatin'.

The simplest solutions are often the best. Hold that slippery skin with a paper towel and pull it away from the chicken body. Of course, if you're makin' Momma Paula's Southern fried chicken, girl, you'll want to leave that skin on right where it grows naturally.

■ Get rid of my garlic breath so when the guests kiss good-bye, they don't stagger away?

Parsley. Chewin' parsley cleans the breath. Fennel seeds work, too.

Salt is mentioned in the Bible

more times than any other spice or food.

SIX PANS YOU CAN'T LIVE WITHOUT

■ A stock pot for makin' soup, boilin' corn, and cookin' pasta. If it has a steamer basket, you can also use it to steam fresh veggies and shellfish.

■ A cast-iron skillet is one of the best cookin' utensils you can ever invest in. If it's handed down from your grandmomma, that makes it even better. There's almost nothin' you can't do in it: sauté, braise, and fry—and you can use it as a roasting or baking pan, too.

■ An enameled cast-iron Dutch oven with a tight-fittin' lid, for braising those short ribs and slow cookin' stews and soups.

■ A roasting pan for roasting meat and poultry, as well as baking lasagna. Many come with a rack that elevates the meat from sittin' in the drippin's.

■ An omelet pan with a flat bottom and a long handle.

■ A boiler, which is a 2- to 4-quart saucepan with a cover. It's nothin' but a pot with a handle, and you'll use it for cooking veggies, rice, soup, and sauces.

COOKIN' FIRST AID

DISASTER: I oversalted the soup.

FIRST AID: Throw in some raw potatoes and fish em' out when they're cooked. The potatoes absorb the salt.

DISASTER: My gravy is lumpy.

FIRST AID: Strain the gravy, then run it through a food processor or a blender to smooth it out. Or just take a whisk and beat that baby to a pulp.

DISASTER: My gravy is too thin.

FIRST AID: Mix a little cornstarch 'n' cold water together and make a slurry, then add it to the boilin' gravy, which will tighten it up. Some like to go back and add more flour, but I find that flour added at this point makes the gravy knotty and lumpy.

DISASTER: My French fries are soggy.

FIRST AID: Honey, I can *so* fix that. To make the best French fries, you want to cut your potatoes and fry 'em in deep hot grease for about two or three minutes. Bring them out with a slotted spoon and put 'em on a cookie sheet lined with paper towels or a brown paper grocery sack. You can do that three or four hours ahead of time. When you're ready to pull your meal together, put the potatoes back in the fryer or the pan (again in deep hot grease) for about five minutes or until golden brown. Tip: Don't overcrowd your pan or fryer, 'cause if you do, you're gonna get some white 'n' soft fries (which, frankly, I love anyway).

DISASTER: The muffins stick to the pan.

FIRST AID: You wanna make sure that you first spray your muffin tins real good or use paper cupcake liners. Still, I've had cakes or muffins that stuck. When that happens, take a real cold wet rag, squeeze out most of the water, and sit your muffin tins or cake pans on the rag. It will help shrink the muffins so you can pull 'em loose.

DISASTER: I overcooked the rice.

FIRST AID: You *could* stir in some finely chopped onion or celery and some chicken broth to freshen up the rice, but why not just start with Minute Rice? Oh, I know the Food Snobs are gonna have conniptions, but you cannot screw up Minute Rice *if* you salt the water and throw in some butter. If you like a stickier rice or you have a Food Snob coming for dinner, use less water than the recipe calls for so the rice will clump together. I promise you, no one will guess it's Minute Rice.

DISASTER: I cut up my fruit for fruit salad and it's yucky brown two hours before dinner.

FIRST AID: Sprinkle those babies with lemon juice, cover with plastic wrap, and they'll be pretty and fresh for serving.

Fried chicken is the most popular meal ordered in

American sit-down restaurants. Next come roast beef,

spaghetti, turkey, baked ham, and fried shrimp.

Sounds like a regular day at the Deen household.

GERMAN CHOCOLATE CAKE BARS

*I*rresistible bites of gooey deliciousness! Cut your squares big for a dessert-size portion or smaller if you're serving a crowd.

Crust:

One 18-ounce box chocolate, Swiss chocolate, or devil's food cake mix (not one with pudding added!)

½ cup (1 stick) unsalted butter, melted

1 large egg

Filling:

One 14-ounce can reduced-fat sweetened condensed milk

1 teaspoon vanilla extract

1 large egg

1 cup chopped pecans

1 cup sweetened shredded coconut

½ cup milk chocolate chips

1. Preheat the oven to 350°F. Grease a 13 by 9-inch baking pan well with butter.

2. In a medium bowl, mix together the cake mix, butter, and egg, and press into the bottom of the prepared pan. The crust should not come up the sides. Bake for 7 minutes and remove from the oven. The crust will not look done.

3. While the crust is baking, in a medium bowl mix together the condensed milk, vanilla, egg, pecans, and coconut. Pour evenly over the warm crust and sprinkle evenly with the chocolate chips. Bake for 24 to 30 minutes, until the top is a light golden brown. Remove from the oven and cool completely before cutting into squares.

MAKES ONE 13 BY 9-INCH PAN

THE BAG LADY'S
SANDWICH SECRETS

Seems like another lifetime ago that I was The Bag Lady, sellin' sandwiches door to door in little bags. I'm still makin' the best sandwiches on the planet, and this is how:

■ Put your favorite tuna salad in pita bread pockets and sprinkle a handful of bean sprouts over the tuna.

■ I truly love chicken salad sandwiches topped with ripe avocado slices.

■ Love, love, love cooked peppers on top of almost any sandwich filling.

■ Ain't nothin' a Southerner likes better than a plain old tomato sandwich made with whole-wheat on the bottom and white bread on the top, and flavored with a spread of grated onion, black pepper, and Accent mixed into Hellmann's or Best Foods mayonnaise.

■ Sauté up some onions and mushrooms and put them on your hamburger for a heavenly taste treat. Yummmy.

■ Love, love, love a fried egg on top of my cheeseburgers!

■ Thinly sliced meatloaf, tomatoes, and mayonnaise on toasted sourdough bread puts a hitch in your giddyup!

■ I chop up cold butter into small cubes and work them into my hamburger meat. Then I shape the meat into patties, throw 'em on the grill, and cook 'em to my guests' favorite temperatures. It's as good as steak, y'all.

The pound cake got its name from

the pound of butter it contained.

My kind of cake.

THE PERFECT CAKE

*O*kay, you've baked a honey of a cake. How do you frost it so it don't look like a four-year-old's been at it? Well, the first thing you want to do is cut you off four strips of waxed paper, about three inches wide each. Lay the strips down on the rim of the plate in a square with a smallish open space in the middle and the strips kinda overlapping the rim. Then you put down your first layer of cake, and frost over the top of it. Next, lay your top layer down on the first layer with the top of the top shmushed into the frosting and the nice, flat bottom stickin' up, and you're ready for the good part.

I must tell you there's controversy on whether you frost the sides first, or the top first.

I was makin' a hummingbird cake with Martha Stewart on her television show, and I said to her, serious-like, "Martha, I'm gonna ask you a question. I want to know *where* you start when you're frostin' a cake. I've never been schooled, so I don't know what the proper way is."

"I always start with the top," she said. And I said, "I always start with the sides."

And I still think my way is better. Now, a lotta people use frosting spatulas but my momma always used just a big ole spoon and a butter knife. I start by spoonin' out my frostin' just around the edge on top of the cake, then I take my knife and pull that frosting down along the sides of the cake. I do that all the way around the cake, and I save the top till last.

When I'm ready, I just take that knife, dip it first in warm water, then frosting, and swirl, then swirl some more. I dip the butter knife down in the water often, and then just smooth the top of my cake so it looks like a ripple-y pond.

You can be as sloppy as you want with the frosting because when you're all done frosting your cake, just slip out the dripped-on waxed paper strips. You've got a gorgeous cake and a clean plate!

By the way: If you're only bakin' two layers but you want a four-layer cake, slice each of the two layers in half with a piece of dental floss. You'll get two perfect layers from each larger one. Do it while the cake's still warm.

Chocolate contains phenylethylamine (PEA),

a natural substance that's supposed to jog the same reaction

in the body as fallin' in love. Why am I not surprised?

MIZ PAULA,
I WANT TO SEND
CHOCOLATE CHIP COOKIES
TO MY SON AT CAMP.
HOW DO I WRAP THEM
SO THEY DON'T BREAK?

Get yourself some Styrofoam peanuts and a cardboard box from one of those packaging shops. First, gently wrap the cookies in several flat layers, each layer covered with plastic wrap. Put a flat layer of the Styrofoam peanuts in the box, then a layer of the wrapped cookies, than another layer of the Styrofoam peanuts, then another of cookies. Then another, then another. Pack 'em nice and snug so they can't move around. Finish with a layer of the Styrofoam peanuts.

Write FRAGILE on the outside of the box so the cookies don't get thrown in the throw-bin at the post office. I guarantee your son's chocolate chips will arrive intact.

And if they don't? I never yet saw a kid who threw away a broken cookie.

CHICKEN 101

CHICKEN	SIZE	HOW TO COOK
Broiler/fryer	About 2–2½ pounds	You can do anything with it—roast whole, or broil it whole after you've split and flattened the bird; it's also great fried whole in a deep fryer
Roaster	About 3–5 pounds; plumper and fattier than a broiler/fryer	Roast, grill, or smoke whole; boil for wonderful chicken and dumplings or chicken salad
Cornish hen	1–2 pounds; hardly any fat; tender and yummy	Roast whole for individual servings
Capon	4–10 pounds; a small, young rooster with a tender breast	Roast whole
Stewer (also called hen)	5–7 pounds; older and tougher but flavorful; great for stock	Stew, braise, or boil

My momma always said for frying, buy the smallest chicken you can find because those are the youngest and most tender.

HOW MUCH SHOULD I BUY?

*P*robably the easiest way to figure out how much you need of anything for a party is to ask the butcher, the baker, the fishmonger,
the whoever. Just say, "I'm havin' eight for a barbecue. How many ribs do
I buy?"

Here's a chart to give you an idea of what you need to buy for a dinner
party of six hungry people. If you're having six couples, double the
amount, and if they're six real hard-eatin' couples, they'll be happier
than a fat tick on a skinny dog if you triple it; I love havin' leftovers, and
you can usually freeze what you don't eat.

WHAT	HOW MUCH TO BUY
BEEF	
Brisket	8 pounds
London broil	5 pounds
Rib roast, bone-in	8–10 pounds
Filet mignon, sliced into steaks	4–5 pounds
POULTRY	
Chicken parts, bone-in	10 pounds
Boneless chicken breasts, for frying	3–4 pounds
Whole chicken	3 or 4 broilers or roasters
Whole turkey	10–12 pounds
LAMB	
Leg of lamb, bone-in	6–7 pounds
Rack of lamb	3 racks
Lamb chops	2 chops per person
PORK	
Bacon (for bacon and eggs)	About 2–3 pounds
Boneless ham	About 3 pounds
Spareribs	12 pounds
Pork chops	2 chops per person

WHAT	HOW MUCH TO BUY
FISH AND SEAFOOD	
Fresh flounder, sole, or other fish fillets	3–4 pounds
Scallops	2–4 pounds
Fresh shrimp, mussels, clams, or oysters	70–100 pieces (6–9 dozen)
Live crabs	5–7 pounds
Soup or chowder	1½ gallons
DESSERTS	
Cakes	1 cake
Pies	1 pie
Cookies	1 pound
Ice cream	1–2 quarts

The Pillsbury Bake-Off has been held

every year since 1949.

SPRING SALAD

*T*his refreshing salad may seem simple, but the combination of flavors is very special. It goes great with grilled chicken, pork chops, or shrimp.

2 hearts of romaine, tough outer leaves removed, roughly chopped
1 cup chopped fresh dill
4 scallions or green onions, white and tender green parts, chopped
½ cucumber, peeled, seeded, and thinly sliced

4 large radishes, trimmed, halved, and thinly sliced
⅓ cup crumbled feta cheese

Juice and zest of 1 large lemon
Extra-virgin olive oil
Salt and freshly ground black pepper

1. In a large salad bowl combine the lettuce, dill, scallions, cucumber, radishes, and feta.

2. Place the lemon juice and zest in a glass jar with a tight-fitting lid. Add twice as much olive oil, and salt and pepper to taste. Cover the jar and shake well. Pour the dressing over the salad and gently toss to combine. Serve immediately.

SERVES 6

LEFTOVERS

*B*ein' rich is having leftovers. Good leftovers make yo' tongue fly outta yo' mouth and smack yo' brains out.

If you're lucky enough to have any chicken—or better still, fried chicken—left over, go ahead and pick it off the bone as soon as supper's over. Dice it up. Throw a little mayonnaise in to moisten it and keep it from havin' that leftover refrigerator taste. When you're ready to eat, go ahead and put in your celery, your onions, your boiled eggs, whatever you do to it. Put it on a bed of fresh greens and tomatoes and presto—chicken salad.

Leftover baked fish and plain broiled fish like salmon make wonderful salads or sandwiches.

Leftover vegetables? Oh, Lord, yes. I mean like if I've got creamy mashed potatoes left over? The next day I put an egg in the taters and a little bit of flour and diced onion and make fried potato patties. And, of course, you sure never wanna throw away even one smidgen of green beans, turnip greens, collard greens, creamed corn—all that's good for the next day. In fact, turnips and collards, butter beans, and black-eyed peas, they just get better the second time around.

You can always put those leftover veggies in a soup. If you have, say, a half a cup of peas left over from a meal, don't throw 'em away. Keep a covered container in your freezer and every time you have a dab left over, even if it's just a couple of tablespoons, throw it in that container. When you're ready to make soup, just pull out that container—the one that's got a dab of this, a dab of that, a dribble of that—and you got a pot of the best vegetable soup you ever tasted.

If I see anyone in my house throwin' out my good leftovers, they're done for. Nobody better get between a fat girl and her food, 'specially if the girl's *me*.

SOUP HEAVEN

I love making potato soup because it takes me back to my momma. I had a chronic strep throat growin' up, and *the* worst tonsils till I was about seventeen. I'd run a temperature of 104 and my throat would hurt so bad. Momma would make me potato soup and I'd just sigh with the pleasure of it. I made the same soup whenever Bobby and Jamie were sick.

Now, I like meat in my soups, so I always add a little ham, and I make the best vegetable-beef soup on the planet with good ole short ribs and serve it with corn bread . . . well, ain't yo' mouth waterin' right now?

Here's somethin' else: I never met a Campbell's soup I didn't like. The Food Snobs certainly look down their nose at canned soups, but you know, I can't operate without 'em. My grandmomma didn't make a pot of chicken 'n' dumplin's that didn't have Campbell's Cream of Celery soup in it because it helped give the chicken 'n' dumplings a little bit o' thickness and flavor.

The word "soup" comes from the Middle Ages word sop,

which means a piece of bread over which the first roast

drippins' were poured. The main ingredient in soup in

6000 B.C. (the first archaeological mention of soup) was

hippopotamus bones. Now, that would be one hearty soup.

BREAD

*O*h, my gosh, I love bread. I love crusty bread that I can pull apart and just slather that butter all down in the creases and everywhere it tore, you know?

One of my secrets to pullin' together a meal quickly is keepin' frozen breads in my freezer.

Sometimes, good crusty bread'll have these tiny holes in them and it don't bother me a bit, it just leaves the mayonnaise a place to ooze out.

If I'm havin' spaghetti or lasagna, I love the French bread that's got the real crispy, hard outside. That crunchy, buttery texture just goes so good with Italian dishes. For sandwiches, I love the softer breads.

I think I could probably live on bread and soup.

SOUTHERN COMFORT

*E*verybody's got to know how to make gravy. Everybody don't.

Maybe my favorite comfort food of all time is country-fried steak 'n' gravy. Oh, it's so filling. And you cook the steak down in that brown gravy and it gets so tender, you can cut it with a fork and just pile it on hot buttered rice and corn bread. It don't get no better than that.

I'll never forget the first time I made gravy. I had gone down to Winter Haven, Florida, to spend a couple of weeks with my Grandmomma and Grandpoppa Hiers. One afternoon, Grandmomma had gone to the grocery store or church or somethin' and Grandpoppa was startin' supper. And he said, "I'm gonna make gravy." I said, "Oh, Grandpoppa, teach me how to make that gravy. Let me make that gravy."

I made the biggest mess of it. It was so thick it was like glue, which is why I understand when some people say that gravy is a real problem for 'em.

But you know what, honey? Gravy is one of the easiest things in the world to make. Say you're havin' fried chicken or pork chops or any meat that you've floured and fried. You want to pour off that grease except for about a third of a cup, and also leave all those little crunchies in the bottom of your pan. Sprinkle about three tablespoons of all-purpose flour in the pan, add some salt and pepper, and cut your heat down to about medium. Then you let that flour brown as you constantly stir it with a wooden spoon. You add your water—a cup and a half or two cups—and let it all come to a roilin' boil.

Turn down the heat and let it simmer for a few minutes. You can add more water if you need to, or if it's too thin, you can mix a little cornstarch in cold water, bring the gravy back up to a roilin' boil, and add the mix; that'll tighten it up. You can also throw you a tablespoon of butter into your gravy if you want to. I do.

You know, there's nothin' better than two pieces of fresh white bread with butter smeared on 'em, covered in gravy. You can make a meal out o' that. And when you fry up some country steak in that gravy, you'll think you died and went to heaven.

BUTTER

*M*ichael said one day that I was the only person he knew who put butter in her cornflakes. (Not true, by the way.) Jamie says that people think I'm tied to an IV line of butter, but the truth is I believe in all things, including butter, in moderation. I don't use tons of butter, even though it sounds like I do.

It seems to me that all this emphasis on stoppin' enjoying yourself, on constant *restriction*, has made us a nation of resentful people. Folks need to break out sometimes, even if it ain't great for them. Butter in moderation ain't bad when you compare it to a couple of beers or hittin' the dog. You know, I am so sick of cuttin' on my television and everyone on it is obsessed with livin' forever. Well, I have got a news flash: Ain't none of us gettin' out o' here alive. And the time that I do have here, I want to enjoy it, but I'm saying moderation. Live life a little on the edge. Have *some* butter on that biscuit.

Oh, I would be *so* teed off if I didn't put butter on my biscuit one mornin' and I walk out there and a truck hits me. And there my ass is, lyin' out in that street to die healthy. Oh, nooo, darlin'.

Salted or unsalted?

Now, if you ask chefs what they use in cookin'—salted or unsalted?—every last one will tell you unsalted, but I particularly love salted butter. I go to a fancy restaurant and they bring this unsalted stuff to the table and I taste it 'cause I'm polite—and it's too damn bland. So I get me a salt shaker and then I'm just as happy as if I had good sense. Chefs will tell you especially to use the unsalted in bakin'. Not me; I love that contrast between the sweet and the salty; we get along like a house on fire.

Can I use whipped butter in a recipe calling for butter?

That dawg won't hunt. Whipped butter is full of air. By the way, when you're bakin', even using light butter can really make a dish fail.

What's clarified butter?

Clarifying butter is simply removing the water from the butter. If you're havin' crab legs, you don't want to dip those legs down into a watery mess, right? Just put that butter in a pot and boil it gently till the water has evaporated, or melt the butter, then take a ladle and skim off the oily part of the butter; in the bottom of the pan, you'll see milky-lookin' stuff—that's what you throw out.

Flavored Butters

I love makin' flavored butters. You can make savory butters, you can make sweet butters, you can do a dill butter, you can make a basil butter, you can make a strawberry butter, you can make a crab butter . . . there's no end. And they make the greatest little gifts at Christmastime. You can go to antique shops or yard sales and find pretty little ole glass containers and fill 'em with your flavored butters and put bows on 'em and they make great gifts.

You can freeze 'em, too; it's like money in the bank. Place the soft butter in parchment paper, shape it into a log, then wrap it in the parchment paper. Finally, wrap the whole log in plastic wrap and throw it in the freezer. Pull it about half an hour before you need it and put a big old slice on your steak or on your piece o' fish.

BUSY-DAY CHICKEN

*T*his dish tastes like you've been cooking all day, but it couldn't be easier: just put all the ingredients in one pot, cover it, and walk away till it's done. You can cook this on top of the stove or in a slow cooker (see Notes). Make it with your favorite parts of the bird and serve it with rice or egg noodles and some steamed green beans. You've got a dinner that will please everyone.

3 pounds bone-in chicken parts, skin removed, rinsed
One 2-ounce envelope onion soup mix

2 tablespoons dark brown sugar
One 15-ounce can plain tomato sauce (or two 8-ounce cans)

In a large skillet or saucepan, place the chicken parts and sprinkle evenly with the onion soup mix and brown sugar. Pour the tomato sauce over all. Turn the heat to medium-high and cook until the mixture just starts to bubble around the edges, then turn down the heat to medium-low and cover. Cook for 35 to 40 minutes, or until the chicken is done.

Notes:

To make this in a slow cooker, cook on low for 4 hours or high for 2 hours.

If you're feeding a crowd, use one 15-ounce can of tomato sauce and 2 tablespoons of dark brown sugar for every three pounds of chicken. Do not increase the amount of onion soup mix. The cooking time should be about the same.

SERVES 4

PAULA DEEN'S
RORSCHACH TEST

I happen to think the contents of a refrigerator reveals more about a person than one of those psychology Rorschach tests. For instance, my refrigerator says that I'm not home to cook very often because it's filled with nothin' but condiments—stuff that folks send me.

I get real scared if I open someone's refrigerator and there's nothin' but skim milk, fat-free dressin', light sour cream, and low-fat mayonnaise, because it tells me that person doesn't like to cut loose, ya know? No fun at all.

If things are in real small containers and are very, very well organized, then that tells me I'm not goin' to find generous portions and big pots of good food when I show up at her house for dinner. People who don't cook generously are more conservative. That ain't me.

And if I find mold and spoiled food and opened cans without covers and a funny smell in someone's refrigerator when I'm lookin' for a can of soda—well, I'm going to be too plumb busy to go to her barbecue.

ICED TEA

To make the best iced tea, use at least twice as much tea as you would for hot tea—two bags per cup—those ice cubes dilute the strength something fierce. If you're using loose tea, use about two generous teaspoons of tea per cup (then add two more teaspoons for the pot). Don't steep the tea for more than five minutes or it'll be bitter. Add ice cubes (maybe with fresh berries in them), sugar to taste, top with a sprig of mint—and you got yourself a fit glass of iced tea for a sultry Southern summer afternoon.

You can freeze berries into ice cubes

for really pretty iced tea.

FALLBACK FOOD

*I*t's a law of nature: Hungry folk will always stop by when you have nothing in the fridge. Here's some fallback food Michael and I always have in our home for the unexpected and "I wouldn't mind a bite to eat" guest.

First of all, my fabulously creative right-hand man, Brandon Branch, reminds me that every Southern lady keeps a block of cream cheese and a jar of red or green pepper jelly in the refrigerator. You spread some pepper jelly on a slab of cream cheese, put out some crackers—and you have an appetizer or hors d'oeuvre that took all of sixty seconds to prepare.

I also always have pimiento cheese in my refrigerator to serve as a dip with good crackers or bread, or stuffed into celery. I drain and chop the pimientos that come in handy four-ounce jars, mix them with grated sharp Cheddar or Monterey Jack cheese, a dash of dry mustard, a taste of vinegar, and some mayonnaise; it's so good and can be made weeks in advance and kept in the refrigerator.

Michael and some of his pals who regularly drop in (including one of his best friends whose name is Buckethead) love a twice-baked potato with shrimp mashed up in it, so I usually keep a couple of those in my freezer. Sometimes I freeze some cooked steaks. I pull out those potatoes and serve them with the steaks and a vegetable. The whole gang of uninvited people are speechless. A whole meal that comes out of the kitchen faster than green grass through a goose? You got it.

You know what else I always keep in my freezer? Frozen biscuits. I can throw those biscuits in the oven and fry up some eggs 'n' bacon and I got the whole meal in twelve minutes.

Oh, and I always, always, always keep a nice presliced Smithfield ham.

I think folks get better eatin's when they just drop by than when I'm expectin' them.

MY SIX MOST *SERIOUS* COOKIN' RULES

1. Read the recipe through, *all the way through,* before you start.

2. Be familiar with cookin' terms and what they mean. *Stir* doesn't mean *fold. Dice* doesn't mean *chop. Scald* doesn't mean *boil.* It makes a huge difference.

3. Clean up as you go along. To me, a meal tastes better if my kitchen is not a mess. Finished with the bowl? Rinse it and put it in the dishwasher.

4. Taste as you cook, and don't end up puttin' your dish on the table undersalted. Let your own tongue be the judge. Say you're makin' spaghetti sauce—the recipe you're following may not suit your taste, so you'll need to put more oregano in than the recipe calls for. You'll only know what you're missin' if you taste as you go.

5. Use good ingredients. You can't take a sow's ear and make a silk purse from it. I may be famous for usin' prepared foods, but if I'm goin' to use canned English peas, I'm usin' the best canned English peas. If I'm usin' mayonnaise, it ain't gonna be salad dressing, it ain't gonna be a cheap mayonnaise, it's gonna be a good mayonnaise.

6. Don't turn up your nose at quality convenience foods. I rarely meet a cake mix I don't love. Frozen biscuits, pizza dough, piecrusts, and, oh my, frozen dumplings—put the woman who invented them on a pedestal!

USE IT OR LOSE IT!

I know a whole lot of people who keep their best dishes and silver in a cupboard, only to be opened for the dustin', which is about as useful as a back pocket on a shirt.

The beautiful crystal bowl your momma left you? It would be perfect for the fried corn you're serving at the barbecue. The precious sterling silver your grandmomma got as a weddin' present? Polish it up, put it out, and make your family Sunday breakfast special. In the South, most of us use our good stuff every day. I've said a thousand times, if my family can't touch it, then I really don't want it; I don't want to feel I'll fall apart if somebody breaks it.

Use your best stuff; it makes the cookin' taste better.

Plastic bags from the supermarket

seemed to take over the kitchen. Then I

learned to take the tube out of a roll of

paper toweling and shove the plastic

bags in there—away and out of sight.

A SOUTHERN SUNDAY MORNIN'

*M*ake yourself a typical Southern breakfast of:

Grits

Buttermilk biscuits (Frozen, I'm not ashamed to say.)

Eggs

Fried fish (It's so stinkin' good for breakfast.)

Fish roe (My momma used to cook us fish roe: the female is the orange stuff but I loved the male stuff best, which I now know is actually sperm . . . can't hardly find it anymore.)

Fried country ham with red-eye gravy (Take the ham out of the pan and pour water in the hot pan to loosen up all the little bits that are left from the fryin'. Then pour in about a half a cup of good strong black coffee. There's a fine chance you won't need salt. Maybe a little pepper and a tablespoon of butter. That's it: red-eye gravy, children. Goes over the ham and the grits and tastes like gravy from the gods.)

After you've had this breakfast, you're practically born Southern.

The average ear of corn has eight hundred

kernels arranged in sixteen rows.

IT AIN'T ALL
ABOUT THE COOKIN'

*E*very great dinner party is also about the conversation, y'all, if you only ask the right questions.

Here are three questions guaranteed to get your dinner partner chatterin'.

1. *What was your first job?* (Everyone's had one. Everyone likes to tell about it.)

2. *What was your favorite meal in yo' momma's house?*

3. *What is the best joke you heard lately?*

A piece of French toast that was partially eaten by

Justin Timberlake was sold on eBay. Hmmm.

Wonder how much Michael's unfinished oxtails

would be worth? Oh, wait a minute—there ain't

never no unfinished oxtails.

Mayonnaise is a great skin moisturizer.

MIZ PAULA, I HAVE THIS TINY, CRAMPED KITCHEN. HOW CAN I COOK GREAT MEALS FOR MORE THAN ONE GUEST?

There are ways to work in a cramped kitchen. I remember when we first moved to Savannah and there wasn't any money for the stove I wanted. I put a hot meal on the table every night with an electric fryin' pan; I went to Wal-Mart and I bought me a double burner so that I could boil my peas. You can make do.

Get organized: You have to get a magnetic rack for your cookin' knives. Pots and large utensils can live on hooks or a rack on the wall. Put up some inexpensive metal or wooden shelving units to store your appliances; instead of a stand mixer, use a hand mixer; get a mini food processor instead of a full-sized one. Store big boxes on top of the refrigerator.

Make counter space: Pull out a cabinet drawer and put a tray on it. When I was operatin' The Bag Lady, I had this small kitchen with maybe four feet of counter space, and I was puttin' together 200, 250 meals every mornin'. I told Jimmy Deen, my husband at the time, "I have just got to have more counter space," so he went and bought some flat wood and two-by-fours, and made me a platform that rested on the top of the stove. When I got done with all my cookin', I put that on top of the stove and that extended my counter space about three or four feet. When I was done, I'd take it off and stow it away. Where there's a will, there's a way.

De-clutter: The ice cream machine, your momma's Limoges china, the salad spinner, the espresso machine, the fabulous statue you bought at a garage sale—when you have a larger kitchen, *then* you can invite them all back home.

Get the most out of what you have: **One item, many uses. Think toaster oven. Use it for toasting, roasting, and broiling. Use a small fingernail brush for cleaning graters, colanders, and garlic presses.**

Clean up as you go: **Store dirty dishes in the dishwasher instead of wasting valuable counter space. If you have no dishwasher, put them in the sink filled with sudsy water. Put a trash can right near so you can dispose of stuff you don't need the minute you don't need it.**

Don't sweat the teeny junk: **Set up a basket to dump junk mail, memo pads, keys, clips, messages, bills, pencils—anything that finds its way to the kitchen but may not, by your orders, live on a counter.**

An etiquette writer of the 1840s said,

"Ladies may wipe their lips on the

tablecloth, but not blow their noses on it."

DEEP-FRYIN': THE BASICS

*D*eep-fryin' at home in a pan is a challenge, which is why I always advise people to get a deep fryer. There are good small counter-top models, and bigger ones that can be dropped down right into your counter. Most people think deep fryers are only for restaurants, but it's wonderful to have one in your home for everything you fry. Of course, you can always do like my grandmomma did and use a sturdy black cast-iron skillet with about an inch of the grease you choose.

1. The number one rule of deep-frying is that you maintain an even temperature during the fryin', and 350°F is perfect. If you don't put your chicken or whatever you're frying in very hot grease, the crust will fall off, and it will never be crispy or juicy.

2. It's crucial to let your chicken or pork chops or oysters or whatever you're going to fry come to room temperature before frying. If you put cold food into the hot grease, the temperature in the fryer's gonna drop right away, and then you'll get greasy, soggy chicken. Even if the temperature doesn't drop too much right away, it'll drop a little, so make sure you get it back to 350°F. And use gloves—that grease spatters.

3. Make sure your chicken's nice and wet before you flour it. I dip my chicken in beaten egg and hot sauce before I dip it in flour so it sticks real good.

4. Season the food earlier in the day so the seasoning gets a chance to work in there. Mmm—my mouth's waterin' just thinkin' about it!

OVERNIGHT BEANS

This dish comes from my editor's darlin' assistant, Michelle Rorke; it's perfect for a summer barbecue or a hearty winter meal. It's an old family recipe; Michelle's momma makes it in her grandmomma's bean pot, but you can use any ovenproof baking dish.

1 pound dried navy beans
1½ teaspoons salt
½ teaspoon freshly ground black pepper
1 teaspoon dry mustard
A pinch of cayenne pepper

½ cup chopped onion
½ cup molasses
¼ cup dark brown sugar
3 tablespoons cider vinegar
¼ pound salt pork, cubed (optional)

1. Place the beans in a pot and add enough water to cover them by 2 inches. Bring to a boil and boil for 2 minutes. Remove the pot from the heat, cover, and let the beans soak for 1 hour.

2. Drain the beans, return them to the pot, and add fresh water to cover by at least 1 inch. Return the pot to the heat and bring to a boil. Reduce the heat to low and cook until the beans are tender, about 1 hour.

3. Preheat the oven to 300°F. Turn the beans into a 2-quart casserole with a tight-fitting lid. Add the salt, pepper, mustard, cayenne, onion, molasses, brown sugar, vinegar, and salt pork (if using), and enough additional water to cover the beans. Bake, covered, for 6 hours, stirring occasionally. Add boiling water as needed during baking so the beans don't dry out. They should be saucy but not soupy.

SERVES 8 TO 10

FAST-TRACK RIPENING

*I*f you're like me and you buy some luscious-lookin' fruit at the farmers' market, you just can't wait for those peaches to ripen all by themselves. You can always hustle things along. Here's how:

To ripen nectarines, peaches, apricots, avocados, kiwi, mangoes, pears, and plums, place them in a loosely closed brown paper sack. Even avocados ripen faster this way. Plastic bags don't work—they collect moisture that makes the fruit rot.

When is it ripe? You'll know when something is ripe because the fruit will smell sweet and delicious and feel soft but not squishy.

Contrary to popular belief, you shouldn't

store butter in the refrigerator, which

hardens it up and messes with the taste. My

breakfast table always has butter dishes with

sticks of soft butter livin' in them.

MESS AROUND
WITH THE RECIPE

I hope y'all take chances every now and then with your cookin'. It's not written in stone that you got to follow a recipe to the letter. I always say follow it perfectly the first time so you'll know what the recipe writer had in mind, but after that, make it your own.

Some of your family's favorite foods could have very well come out by accident. My friend Katie Lee Joel sent me a copy of her cookbook, *The Comfort Table*. Love, love, love Katie, and I love her deviled eggs. I had a hankerin' for those eggs, so I just looked at the ingredients and didn't pay any attention to the instructions like I tell everybody to do. I said to myself, "Dad gum, you know, she calls for vinegar. I hope it won't make it too juicy. I'm just not gonna put in as much as she calls for."

Well, next time I saw Katie I said, "Did I mention I made your deviled eggs and I thought they were just the best deviled eggs I've ever eaten. Even though I was a li'l concerned about adding vinegar to the filling."

She looked at me funny and she said, "Vinegar?! Vinegar is for the water to boil the eggs in."

Well, I felt dumber than a box of rocks, but I told her, "Well, girl, you just gotta try those deviled eggs when you put a little vinegar *in* 'em."

PUT SOME SOUTH IN YO' MOUTH

*E*very Southern girl knows as soon as she hits the cradle that grits is the mother food. They're ground from dried white or yellow corn, and I think the best are stone-ground. Grits can be happily flavored, used as an entree, an appetizer, a side fixin', and even a fabulous dessert.

THINGS YOU GOTTA KNOW ABOUT FIXIN' GRITS

First of all, use a tall, wide pot. The number one golden rule to cookin' grits is to salt the water *before* you put in the grits, 'cause if you don't salt the water first, you just about can't never get your grits salty enough once they're done cookin'.

The number two rule is you have to stir your grits for about two to three minutes, until every grit is nice and saturated, after you add 'em to your boilin' water. If you don't, you'll end up with golf-ball-size hunks of grits.

Rule number three: In order to cook good, creamy grits, you gotta have a whole stick o' butter in that water. You heard me.

Rule number four: No, rule number one is you never, ever, ever, never use instant grits. I do use quick-cooking grits, but even then, I let those quick grits cook for about thirty minutes. If I had the regular cooking grits, I would cook them for about forty-five minutes.

At the end of my cookin' I always add a little heavy cream or milk. If I'm cookin' grits for a dinner entree, I like to cook 'em in chicken stock instead of water—it gives 'em great flavor.

There ain't nothin' no better than cheese grits. And if I really wanna get fancy, I'll add a can of chopped tomatoes with chile peppers (I use Rotel).

If you have leftover grits, put 'em in a loaf pan, a can, or a drinking glass and store them in your refrigerator. The next morning, slice those grits and fry 'em up. That's beautiful eatin'.

YO' MOMMA

*I*n our restaurant The Lady & Sons, my boys are my partners. I can always outvote them, though, because I may be your partner but I'm still yo' momma.

In the South, being yo' momma trumps all.

I remember once hearing Jamie say to a fan, "Boy, be nice to yo' momma. Someday she may be writin' yo' paycheck."

Momma Always Said

▓ Eatin' oysters will put lead in your pencil.

▓ Let it sit! For the best fried chicken, don't wait to season it just before you start cookin'. Instead, wash and season the bird the morning you're preparing it for dinner, then throw it into the refrigerator, seasoned. It will have time to soak up all the goodness before the cookin'.

▓ Eat the heel of the bread—it'll make you rich!

▓ Take what you'll eat but be sure you eat what you take.

▓ No one has ever gone astray by asking herself, "What if I deep-fried that?"

▓ Collard greens are nature's broom.

▓ Eat plenty of fish—it's brain food, y'all.

▓ Too many cooks can spoil the pot.

▓ A house with no salt is a poor man's house.

▓ If you sing before breakfast, you'll cry before supper.

▓ Don't share a nightmare before your breakfast or it will come true.

▓ Don't eat where you poop and don't poop where you eat.

HOW LONG WILL IT KEEP SO IT DON'T KILL YOU?

*I*f you wrap food real well in silver foil or freezer paper, it will last longer and prevent freezer burn. No food lasts forever, honey, and that goes double for leftovers, which sometimes don't even last a mayfly's day. If *you* want to last, pay attention.

THE FOOD	IN THE REFRIGERATOR (37°–40°F)	IN THE FREEZER 0°F
Meat: lamb, veal, chicken, turkey, pork	3–5 days	4–6 months
Chops	3–5 days	4–6 months
Ground meats	1–2 days	3 months
Ham (fully cooked, whole)	1 week	1–2 months
Lean fish (cod, flounder, sole)	1–2 days	3–6 months
Fatty fish (salmon, bluefish, mackerel)	1–2 days	2–3 months
Bread	(best stored at room temp)	3 months
Cake	(best stored at room temp)	About 3 months
Baked pies	3–4 days	About 1 month
Eggs in their shells	4–5 weeks	Don't freeze
Butter	1–3 months	6–9 months
Whipped butter	1–3 months	Doesn't freeze
Cream (half-and-half)	3–4 days	4 months
Cheese (soft)	1–2 weeks	About 6 months
Cheese (hard)	About 6 months	About 6 months
Cottage cheese, ricotta	1 week	Don't freeze
Ice cream	Don't refrigerate	1–2 months
Yogurt	1–2 weeks	1–2 months

A note on canned food: Store high-acid canned foods like fruit juice or tomatoes on your shelves for up to eighteen months. Vegetables and meats in sealed cans can be stored on shelves for two to five years. Don't even think about buyin' cans that are leaking, dented, or bulging: there's trouble inside. And if it smells funny when you open it, all bets are off and it goes in the trash.

Onions, tomatoes, and potatoes live best on a shelf in your pantry. The refrigerator ruins the taste of a tomato; they turn waxy tastin'. A potato turns sweet in the cold. Onions lose their best pungency in the refrigerator (of course, after I cut 'em, I put 'em in the fridge). Ketchup shouldn't go in the fridge, nor should olive oil. Butter flavor lasts best and longest when the butter's in a covered butter dish outside the fridge; it picks up all kinds of strange flavors in the fridge.

And, of course, mold shouldn't live in your refrigerator. But that's another story.

HOMEMADE MAYONNAISE

Y'all know how I feel about mayonnaise! I go through jars of the stuff, but sometimes there's just nothin' like homemade to make a perfect BLT, as a dippin' sauce for raw veggies, or with a beautiful piece of broiled fish.

There are a thousand ways to make this recipe your own: use lime or orange juice instead of lemon; add whatever chopped-up herbs you like; add some capers, or pickle relish, or salsa—you get the picture!

If you're worried about using raw eggs (which should never be eaten by the very young, the very old, pregnant women, or anyone with a compromised immune system), pasteurized eggs work just fine.

1 egg
1 tablespoon fresh lemon juice
1 teaspoon prepared mustard
½ cup vegetable oil, such as canola

½ cup olive oil
¼ teaspoon salt
A pinch or two of white pepper
A pinch of cayenne or a dash of hot sauce

1. In a blender or food processor fitted with the steel blade, blend the egg, lemon juice, and mustard for about 30 seconds. While the machine is running, add the oil in a slow, steady stream until the mixture is emulsified and thickened. Add the salt, pepper, and cayenne and pulse once or twice to blend.

2. This can be stored in the refrigerator, covered, for 1 week.

MAKES ABOUT 1½ CUPS

COOKIN' WORDS

*G*otta know what cookin' terms mean if you're going to follow a recipe with any degree of success. Here's my idea of a short glossary of the best cookin' words I know.

The Words and What I Think They Mean

Al dente: Vegetables or pasta cooked very lightly, so there's a little bite but not a crunch

Baste: To spoon pan drippings or fat over food as it cooks

Beat: To stir or whip vigorously in a circular motion

Blanch: To cook food (usually fruits and veggies) in boiling water for about 30 seconds, then plunge into ice water. This sets color, loosens skin, or seals juices.

Blend: To combine two or more ingredients or flavors with a blender, whisk, or spoon until everything is nicely merged

Boil: To cook till it bubbles big. When I say *bawl,* I mean boil; I know my Yankee friends pronounce it different!

Braise: To cook food in a bit of liquid, tightly covered, after you've lightly browned it

Chop: To cut food so it's about the size of peas and more coarse than if it were minced

Cream: To beat into a creamy consistency. I cream my butter with sugar for bakin'.

Cut in: To incorporate cold solid fat into a dry ingredient (like flour) till it looks a mess of coarse crumbs. I like to use my fingertips for cuttin' in the butter to the flour, but you can use two knives.

Dice: To cut into tiny squares or cubes

Drippings: The fat, bits and pieces, and juices left in the pan after the meat has cooked

Fold: To combine a light, airy mixture (like beaten egg whites) with a heavier one (like custard). Nice and slow, please. This ain't like beating. Folding works best with a rubber spatula.

Julienne: Veggies cut into thin matchstick forms. These are great for stir-fryin' or garnishes.

Knead: To mix dough (usually with your hands) till it's in a cohesive form. Work that dough till it's pliable.

Mess of: A lot of somethin'. We Southerners, says my Michael, are the only ones who know exactly how much *a mess of* is, and it's too hard to explain. I caught a mess of fish. I ate a mess of collards.

Mince: To cut food in tiny pieces (tinier than chopped)

Puree: To blend until smooth and lump-free. Kinda looks like baby food. *Is* baby food.

Reduce: To cook slowly so liquid evaporates. Flavor becomes so intense!

Sauté: To cook quickly in a small amount of fat or oil in a skillet

Scald: To dip tomatoes or plums (or whatever) into boilin' water for a minute. Makes it real easy to peel them.

Sear: To brown briefly over high heat to lock in juices

Simmer: To cook in liquid, gently. You'll see small, occasional bubbles around the edges of the pan and across the surface.

Stir: To mix slowly with a spoon. Stirring's not blending or beating.

Truss: To tie chicken or other meat with twine or skewers so it holds its shape during cookin'

BUTTERMILK!— Y'ALL CAN MAKE IT YOURSELF!

*O*ften, you'll get in the middle of makin' a recipe and it'll call for buttermilk, and if you're like me, you don't keep buttermilk on hand all the time. That's easy enough to fix: For each cup of buttermilk called for in a recipe, instead use one cup milk and about two tablespoons of any acid like white vinegar or lemon juice. Let it all set for about five minutes and you got buttermilk.

I love to serve a meal I've prettied up with garnishes like a sprig of parsley, a sprinkle of chives on potatoes, bell peppers cut into flower shapes, a maraschino cherry on top of ice cream, or edible flowers tossed on top of a shrimp salad. But Michael ain't one for garnishes. He always says, "Keep the parsley, Paula, and gimme another shrimp."

ZEST

*Z*est is the thin, brightly colored outside skin of citrus fruits that gives intense, powerful, punchy flavor to so many foods from lamb and chicken to cheesecake and muffins. Buy a citrus zester for when the recipe calls for zest. Underneath the zest is a white membrane layer called *pith* that's real bitter—and you do not want pith in your zest, child, so when you get down to the white, stop zesting the fruit. The average lemon will produce about a tablespoon of zest and the average orange will give you four tablespoons. You can freeze it in plastic freezer bags for about six months.

Never skimp on the flavor when you're cookin' for the kids. Want to see your kids smile like a mule eatin' briars? A little butter in the vegetables can be very, very enticin'. I never skimped on the flavor with Jamie and Bobby, just like my momma never did with me and Bubba. I always seasoned my boys' vegetables just like I'd season them for a grown-up person. One of the first "people foods" my grandson Jack ever ate in my house was a squash casserole. I took that little spoon and put a little bite of it in his mouth, and he said, "Mmm." Didn't add no sugar at all . . . just some butter, a little grated cheese, some onion, salt, pepper, and garlic and I got that "mmm."

THE CAKE BATTER'S ALL MIXED—BUT IT DON'T FIT IN THE PAN

*N*o one has every size of everything. Sometimes you just have to make do with what you got, and if you don't have the size pan or dish called for in the recipe, substitute a pan or pans with at least a similar height and the same volume holding power. To check a pan's volume, fill it with water, and measure that water in a glass measuring cup. The width of the pan is measured from the inside edge to inside edge. The depth is measured from the inside bottom of the pan to the top. If you have a lot more batter from a recipe than will fit in the pan you own, use two smaller pans and adjust the cooking time. If you do use a pan that's smaller *and* deeper than the pan specified in the recipe, give the contents a minute or so longer to bake.

Note: If your pan's not in this list, fill it with water to within a quarter-inch of the top, then measure the volume of water to come as close as you can to the called-for size.

Pan Substitutions

ROUND CAKE PANS
8 by 1½ inches = 4 cups
9 by 1½ inches= 6 cups

SQUARE CAKE PANS
8 by 8 by 2 inches = 6 cups
9 by 9 by 1½ inches = 8 cups
9 by 9 by 2 inches = 10 cups

LOAF PANS
8½ by 4½ by 2½ inches = 6 cups
9 by 5 by 3 inches = 8 cups

SPRINGFORM PANS
9 by 2½ inches = 10 cups
10 by 2¾ inches = 15 cups

BUNDT PAN
10 by 3½ inches = 12 cups

MUFFIN TIN CUPS
2¾ by 1⅛ inches = ¼ cup
3 by 1¼ inches = ⅝ cup

DEEP-DISH PIE PAN
10 by 2 inches = 6 cups

Baking Pan Substitutions by Shape

WHAT YOU CAN BAKE IN THIS PAN	YOU CAN BAKE IN THESE PANS
10 by 13½-inch Bundt	Two 8 by 2-inch rounds
9 by 2-inch round	8 by 2½-inch round *or* 8 by 8 by 2-inch square *or* 15 by 10 by 1-inch jelly-roll
10 by 2-inch round	9 by 9 by 2-inch square
12-cup standard muffin tin	8½ by 4½ by 2½-inch loaf *or* 9 by 1½-inch round *or* 8 by 8 by 1½-inch square

CONVERSIONS

*W*hat if you want to make a recipe that's measured on a metric scale and you haven't the slightest idea how to translate that into U.S. units? Here's how:

Liquid Volume Measures

Metric (ml = milliliter)	U.S.
1 ml	¼ teaspoon
2 ml	½ teaspoon
4 ml	¾ teaspoon
5 ml	1 teaspoon
15 ml	1 tablespoon
50 ml	¼ cup
75 ml	⅓ cup
125 ml	½ cup
150 ml	⅔ cup
175 ml	¾ cup
250 ml	1 cup
473 ml	2 cups (1 pint)
1 liter	1 quart
3.8 liters	4 quarts (1 gallon)

Approximate Dry Weight Measures

Metric	U.S.
14 grams	½ ounce
30 grams	1 ounce
55 grams	2 ounces
85 grams	3 ounces
115 grams	4 ounces (¼ pound)
225 grams	8 ounces (½ pound)
455 grams	16 ounces (1 pound)
1 kilogram	2.2 pounds (35¼ ounces)

And, just for your information, if the recipe calls for:

A cool oven: set your oven at 200°F.

A slow oven: set it at about 300°–325°F.

A moderately hot oven: set it at 350°–400°F.

A very hot oven: set it at 450°–500°F.

INGREDIENT STAND-INS

So it's pouring-down rain, you promised to bake brownies for the bake sale, and there's no unsweetened chocolate in the house. What do you do now?

INGREDIENTS	STAND-INS
Allspice, 1 teaspoon	⅔ teaspoon ground cinnamon plus ⅓ teaspoon ground cloves
Baking powder, 1 teaspoon	1 teaspoon baking soda plus ½ teaspoon cream of tartar
Dry bread crumbs	Equal amount of cracker crumbs or shmushed corn flakes; or oven-dry bread and crust in the blender or food processor
Butter	Equal amount of margarine
Cream cheese	Part-skim ricotta cheese or low-fat cottage cheese, beaten until smooth
Chicken or beef broth, 1 cup	1 chicken or beef bouillon cube dissolved in cup of boiling water
Chopped chives	Minced scallion tops
Chocolate, 1 square unsweetened	3 tablespoons unsweetened cocoa powder blended with 1 tablespoon melted butter
Semisweet chocolate, 1 square	3 tablespoons unsweetened cocoa powder plus 2 tablespoons butter or margarine plus 3 tablespoons sugar
Cornstarch, 1 tablespoon, for thickening	2 tablespoons all purpose flour or 4 teaspoons quick-cooking tapioca
Dates or currants	Dark raisins
Self-rising flour	1 cup all-purpose flour plus 1½ teaspoons baking powder plus ½ teaspoon salt

Gelatin, 3-ounce package, flavored	I tablespoon plain gelatin plus 2 cups fruit juice
Honey, I cup	I¼ cups sugar plus ¼ cup water
Ketchup or chili sauce	⅓ cup tomato sauce plus 2 tablespoons sugar plus I tablespoon vinegar
Shallots	White part of scallions or plain white onion
Sour cream	Equal amount plain yogurt
Sugar, I cup	I cup light brown sugar, packed, or 2 cups confectioners' sugar
Brown sugar, I cup	¾ cup granulated sugar plus ¼ cup molasses
Tomato juice, I cup	½ cup tomato sauce plus ½ cup water
Vinegar, I teaspoon	2 teaspoons lemon juice

AUTUMN APPLESAUCE

*T*his smells so good when it's cooking! The combination of apples, plums, and cinnamon is pretty darn tasty, too. Use whatever apples you have on hand; I like a mix of McIntosh and Granny Smith myself. I serve this as a side with roast chicken or pork, or as dessert with a little heavy cream poured over the top. It's not bad for a snack or breakfast, either.

3 pounds apples, cored and sliced
1 pound Italian blue plums, pitted and sliced
¼ cup light brown sugar, plus additional to taste
2 cinnamon sticks

A pinch of salt
¼ cup water (or cider, apple juice, or orange juice)
1 teaspoon vanilla extract

Put the apples, plums, brown sugar, cinnamon sticks, salt, and water in a large heavy pot over medium heat. Cook, stirring occasionally, until the apples and plums are soft and falling apart, 45 minutes to 1 hour. Remove from the heat, add the vanilla, and taste. If it's not sweet enough for your taste, add brown sugar a tablespoon at a time until it tastes right to you. Cool. Put the applesauce through a food mill. Serve at room temperature or chilled.

MAKES ABOUT 8 CUPS

A FEW WORDS ON KNIVES

■ More people are cut bad with dull knives than with sharp ones.

■ Never buy a set of knives—buy them one knife at a time, so you get exactly what you need. Before you buy, try, preferably on a cutting board.

■ You need at least four good knives for the preparation of food: a small paring knife with a 2- to 4-inch blade, for coring, peeling, and slicing; a chef's knife with an 8- to 10-inch blade for chopping vegetables, mincing garlic, and carving meat; a fillet knife with a thin blade, for deboning meat and poultry and for cleaning fish; and a serrated knife, for neat slicing of bread, loaf cakes, and tomatoes.

■ Take good care of your knives. Never store them in kitchen drawers with a lot of metal junk that inevitably will dull blades. I think butcher blocks are ideal storage. Bad things happen to good knives when you put them in the dishwasher.

■ You can take 'em into a lawn mower store to have the blades sharpened.

PAULA'S SHOPPIN' SECRETS

■ Make friends with the guys behind the fish and meat counters. Ask them what they'd choose for their own dinners, and why they chose it. People love to teach what they know; your best education in food can come from your local butcher or fishmonger. And often they have the freshest fish or chop in the back of the shop. If the merchant likes you, he'll go get that fresh fish for y'all.

■ I love to go to a local farmers' market when I'm buying fruit and veggies. There's nothing like produce right off the land.

■ Fragrance is a better clue to a great tomato than color. Smell the stem end—it should have a fresh, garden-y scent. In the winter months, when it's hard to find a flavorful tomato, I'll switch to a grape tomato, which seems to have a wonderful flavor all year-round. During the summer, I like buyin' my tomatoes in different stages so I have some to eat that day and some that'll be ready to eat three days from now.

■ Buyin' lettuce? If the cut end is deep brown, it isn't real fresh. But all's not lost: just cut off the discolored part and put the lettuce in an ice-water bath; the lettuce will drink that water and get crisp again. Take it out of the water, shake it well, wrap it between a couple of sheets of paper towels or a clean dish towel, and put it in a two-gallon plastic bag in the refrigerator till you're ready to make your salad.

■ Potatoes should be smooth, nicely shaped, firm, and free of those soft, darker dents.

■ Fresh mushrooms are firm and tough but delicate; overripe mushrooms have wide open, pitted, and discolored caps. If I want to stuff mushrooms, I'll go to a grocery that sells them loose by the pound so I can pick out each and every one to be the same size.

■ Green beans should be slender, bright-colored, and crisp—break one to check.

■ Brussels sprouts are brightly colored and their outer leaves fit tightly instead of flopping off.

■ The best-eatin' carrots are smallish, firm, and smooth, without cracks or those grayish rootlets hanging loose (which indicate senior-citizen carrots).

■ Asparagus should be bright, deep green with closed, firm, unmoldy tips. If the spear has long ridges or ribs, it's probably old, tough, and flavorless.

■ I love to husk and silk my fresh corn right in the market (many stores provide a bin for just that purpose) rather than mess up my whole kitchen. I know the Food Police claim that corn should not be husked until the

moment before it's cooked, but I think that's stupid. Look for bright green, moist husks and stiff, moist "silk" when you pick out your ears. I look to see if each corn's filled out real good. I always take my corn and stick my thumbnail in a kernel—if it squirts juice, that's a good piece o' corn. If it don't squirt, go over to the freezer case and buy some frozen.

■ If it's a ripe cantaloupe, when you press your finger where the stem grew, it should give some. It should smell sweet.

■ To tell if it's a ripe honeydew, shake it and smell it. If it's ripe, you'll hear the seeds rollin' around and it should smell sweet.

■ When pineapples are ripe, they have a delicious, strong, pineapple-y fragrance and the leaves on top pull out easily.

■ "If it's fish and it stinks, it stinks," says my Michael, and he knows his fish. A fresh fish will never smell bad. Make sure that the eyes are clear—if they're cloudy, stay away. Check to see that the scales are shiny and the gills red. Trust your instincts and look at the way the fish behind the counter is being presented. If the tuna's been badly cut, if the cod is broken open and sittin' in a pile of fish juice, you know you don't have careful or knowledgeable merchants.

■ Shrimp: If the heads and tails are turnin' black, they're not all that fresh. If the tails are all black, they've already been frozen or they're *really* not fresh.

■ If you buy prepackaged chops or steaks, look for a very tight seal with no pockets of air. Beef should be firm and cool to the touch. Remember that it's "first in, first out" for meat displays: meat in front of the case is not as fresh as the meat in the back of the display. Don't hesitate to ask for a cut from the back. Also, when buying meat from supermarket cases, remember that the lights above are often tinted pink to show that meat to its greatest advantage. Take the meat away from the counter and hold it in the regular store light to see its true color.

■ In fact, "first in, first out" is true of many items, from mushrooms to milk: always buy the ones in the back because the ones in the front will spoil first. Even if items are dated, go for the ones in the back.

■ Always check those expiration dates, y'all! That gallon of milk in the back of the cooler may have a life five days longer than the gallon in the front. With today's high prices, we need to get the biggest bang for our bucks that we can manage.

■ If you are disappointed with any product you bring home, bring it right back. I never visited a market that didn't take back a bad product and apologize for your trouble.

CANDY-MAKING TEMPERATURES

Stage of Candy	Temperature (°F)
Dark caramel	350–360
Medium caramel	338–350
Light caramel	320–338
Hard crack	300–310
Soft crack	270–290
Hard ball	250–266
Firm ball	244–248
Soft ball	234–240
Thread	223–234

MEASURING EQUIVALENTS

1 tablespoon	3 teaspoons
⅛ cup	2 tablespoons
⅓ cup	5 tablespoons plus 1 teaspoon
½ cup	8 tablespoons
⅔ cup	10 tablespoons plus 2 teaspoons
¾ cup	12 tablespoons
1 cup	16 tablespoons
8 fluid ounces	1 cup
1 pint	2 cups
1 quart	2 pints
4 cups	1 quart
1 gallon	4 quarts
16 ounces	1 pound

PAULA'S BAKING PANTRY

With these items in your pantry, whipping up a batch of brownies for the kids after school or a quick dessert when friends come to dinner is a snap.

On your shelves:

- Unbleached all-purpose flour
- Self-rising flour
- Cake flour
- Cornmeal, white and yellow
- Old-fashioned oatmeal
- Baking powder
- Baking soda
- Vegetable shortening
- Vegetable oil
- Chocolate chips: semisweet, milk, and white
- Unsweetened chocolate
- Semisweet chocolate
- White chocolate
- Unsweetened cocoa powder
- Granulated sugar
- Brown sugar, light and dark
- Confectioners' sugar
- Unsulfured molasses
- Pure vanilla extract
- Pure almond extract
- Whole nutmeg (and a nutmeg grater!)
- Cinnamon
- Salt

In your refrigerator:

- Salted and unsalted butter (I like everyday eatin' butter that's not kept in a refrigerator, but if you're storing it for long periods of time, it's best to freeze or refrigerate.)
- Milk
- Buttermilk
- Heavy cream
- Sour cream
- Large eggs
- Oranges
- Lemons
- Limes
- Nuts, especially pecans and almonds

In the freezer:

- Unsweetened frozen fruit (strawberries, blueberries, raspberries, peaches)

PAULA'S PARTY PANTRY

A well-stocked pantry means guests are always welcome. With these things on hand I can go from "guess who's coming to dinner" to "gather round the table" in no time.

On the shelves:

- Canned artichokes
- Canned beans
- Broth: chicken, beef, clam
- Canned salmon
- Canned tomatoes
- Canned tuna
- Pasta and noodles
- Rice
- Salsa
- Crackers
- Herbs and spices
- Salt and pepper
- Garlic
- Onions
- Potatoes
- Honey
- Hot pepper sauce
- Jams, jellies, preserves
- Mustard
- Olive oil
- Peanut butter
- Tomato sauce
- Vegetable oil
- Vinegar
- Coffee
- Tea

In the refrigerator:

- Bacon
- Butter
- Cream and/or half-and-half
- Cheese: cheddar, Swiss, mozzarella, Parmesan
- Eggs
- Lemons
- Limes
- Mayonnaise
- Milk
- Nuts: whole almonds, pecans, cashews
- Olives
- Vegetables: carrots, celery
- Wonton wrappers

In the freezer:

- Ice cream
- Sherbet
- Sorbet
- Peas
- Corn
- Spinach

ACKNOWLEDGMENTS

I give thanks, every day of my life, for . . .

Michael, gorgeous Michael, love of my life—friend, husband, constant delight.

My fabulous, precious family: my handsome sons, Jamie and Bobby, who continually make me so proud I could burst; Jamie's wife, our stunning Brooke; my dream grandson, Jack Deen—the best little jackpot a girl could win; Aunt Peggy Ort and Aunt Trina—my deepest roots; Bubba—my dearest brother and partner—and his wife, Dawn; Bubba's children, Corrie and Jay, and Dawn's sons, Iain and Trevor; Michael's and my beloved Groover kids—Anthony, Michelle, and Michelle's husband, Daniel Reed; Michael's brothers, Father Hank Groover and Nick Groover, and their families are also part of my glorious, extended family.

Sherry Suib Cohen, my New York sister and collaborator who not only talks Southern now, she even cooks Southern—with maybe a bit less *buttah* than I'd recommend. We sit up on my bed and we laugh and we cry and somehow we get my words on paper.

My Savannah team who helped me put together this cookin' journal with heart and organization, especially my gorgeous, witty, brilliant Brandon Branch; Theresa Luckey, the best executive assistant on the planet; the marvelous, magical Michelle White; Cassie Aimar, my delicious personal assistant; my accomplished accountant, Karl Schumacher; my literary agent, Janis Donnaud, who never stops thinking of how she can get me the best deals in the world; my everything-else agent, the indispensable Barry Weiner—I love you, Barry Cuda!; my Lady & Sons restaurant family, especially Dora Charles, Rance Jackson, Dustin Walls, Scott Hopke, Cookie Espinoza, and the rest of the staff, for whom I'm endlessly grateful.

My Simon & Schuster publishing family has come to feel like my blood family. Sydny Miner is the editor every writer dreams of—careful, loving, inspirational, understanding, and just delightful. Michelle Rorke is her wonderful assistant who has now climbed the publishing ladder to become an assistant editor—congratulations, Michelle! Sybil Pincus was the production editor for this book and Suzanne Fass was the copy editor; they both did Simon & Schuster proud. I'm thrilled to be one of the authors under

the direction of the legendary David Rosenthal, the publisher of Simon & Schuster. Tracey Guest, the director of publicity, is the best; she has a direct line to my pal Oprah! My own personal publicist, Nancy Assuncao, doesn't sleep nights because she doesn't stop thinking of wonderful things she can do for me! I owe her so much, and I love and admire her.

My business partners, Pete Booker, Larry Pope, Jim Schloss, and Joe Luter III are really extraordinary.

Who doesn't love the Food Network? My producer, the tall, terrific, and unique Gordon Elliott, discovered me, my cookin', and my love of people. He changed my whole life, nothing less. What do you say to that man? I adore you, Gordon. Doin' my two shows, *Paula's Home Cooking* and *Paula's Party,* is the most fun anyone ever had. Judy Girard, Brooke Johnson, and Bob Tuschman of the Food Network are talent personified.

Thanks to Shân Willis of Wordsmithery for a meticulous transcription.

Finally, everything I ever did and will do I owe to my sweet momma and daddy, Corrie and Earl Hiers, and to my Grandparents Paul and my Grandparents Hiers; they gave their small, Southern cheerleader child abidin' and unconditional love.

They would have loved this cookin' journal. I hope you do.

ABOUT THE AUTHORS

PAULA DEEN is the bestselling author of *It Ain't All About the Cookin'; Paula Deen Celebrates!; Paula Deen & Friends: Living It Up, Southern Style; The Lady & Sons Just Desserts;* and other books. She is the host of the Food Network's *Paula's Home Cooking* and *Paula's Party,* and has appeared on *Good Morning America, Today, Fox and Friends,* and *The Oprah Winfrey Show*. Paula is the founder of The Lady & Sons restaurant and co-owner of Uncle Bubba's Oyster House. She lives with her family in Savannah, Georgia.

SHERRY SUIB COHEN has written twenty-two books for major publishers and was a contributing editor at *McCall's, Rosie, New Woman,* and *Lifetime* magazines. She regularly writes for periodicals, including *Parade, Family Circle, Redbook, Reader's Digest,* and *Ladies' Home Journal*. Cohen is an award-winning member of the American Society of Journalists and Authors and lives with her husband, Larry, in New York City. She makes a great soup.

Subscribe Today!

Paula Deen shares her secrets for transforming ordinary meals into memorable occasions in each issue of *Cooking with Paula Deen* magazine.

• •

recipes — Easy recipes for mouth-watering meals everyone is sure to enjoy.

desserts — Cakes, pies, cookies, and more!

menus — Delight your family and friends with home-cooked meals perfect for holidays or casual get-togethers.

cooking tips — Simplify your life with time-saving techniques.

To order call: **1-877-933-5736**
Order online: **www.CookingWithPaulaDeen.com**

RECIPE CARDS

RECIPE CARDS

RECIPE CARDS

RECIPE CARDS

RECIPE CARDS

RECIPE CARDS

RECIPE CARDS